W9-ANH-301
D0123847

Yarn Happy

30 Traditional Norwegian Designs for Modern Knit & Crochet

Turid Lindeland

SELLERS
PUBLISHING

Published by Sellers Publishing, Inc.
161 John Roberts Road, South Portland, Maine 04106
Visit our Web site: www.sellerspublishing.com
E-mail: rsp@rsvp.com

First published in 2014 as Garnglede i Rosendal by Turid Lindeland
copyright © 2014 CAPPELEN DAMM AS

English translation © 2015 Sellers Publishing, Inc.
All rights reserved.

ISBN 978-1-4162-4563-6
Library of Congress Control Number: 2015930720

Edited by Robin Haywood
Copyedited by Maya Mackowiak Elson
Layouts by Charlotte Cromwell
English translation by Margaret Berge Hartge

Photography by Bodil Haga
Design by Lise Mosveen
Charts by Denise Samson

All trademarks are the property of their respective owners. Rather than include a trademark symbol after every occurrence of a trademarked name, we use names in an editorial fashion only, and to the benefit of the trademark owner, with no intention of infringement of the trademark.

No portion of this book may be reproduced or transmitted in any form, or by any means, electronic or mechanical, including photographing, recording, or by any information and storage retrieval system, without written permission from the publisher.

The instructions, charts, and material lists were carefully reviewed by the author and the editor; however, accuracy cannot be guaranteed. The author and publisher cannot be held liable for errors. Errata will be published on the Web site www.sellerspublishing.com.

10 9 8 7 6 5 4 3 2 1

Printed and bound in China.

Contents

Introduction

I take great delight in knitting. To me, there's nothing better than to sit with some handwork in my lap and watch how the piece comes together: the colors, the patterns, and the design. I vividly remember my first knitting project, a pink sweater complete with a belt for my doll. Since then, I have produced a large quantity and variety of sweaters, socks, throws, and pillows. Yarn, knitting needles, and crochet hooks make me happy, and they all contribute to my own way of relaxing.

While these pages are full of my knitting and crochet projects, this book is really about the journey I took to discover my dream. It is about traveling back in time to discover forgotten handwork techniques and old patterns, and to give them a modern expression. My desire is to create items of high quality with roots in traditional methods. Pieces that are well cared for and used year after year, and that may become heirlooms for generations to come; an alternative to today's use-and-toss mentality.

In 2007, my husband and I purchased the Rosendal Turisthotell in western Norway — this is where my journey began. After several years of renovation, the hotel is now a showcase of our creative endeavors. Many of our undertakings, from the knitted pieces, to the colors we used on our walls, are inspired by a sock pattern (dated from 1887) I found amid the crumbling walls of the hotel. That pattern, and the geographic features that dominate the scenery have guided my designs. The glaciers, fjords, forests, coastline, and mountains: they have informed the color collections seen here in this book.

I hope you will enjoy *Yarn Happy* and that it will prompt you to create memorable moments both with and without yarn in your hands.

– Turid Lindeland

What inspires me . . .

Glaciers

Knee-High Sock Chart S

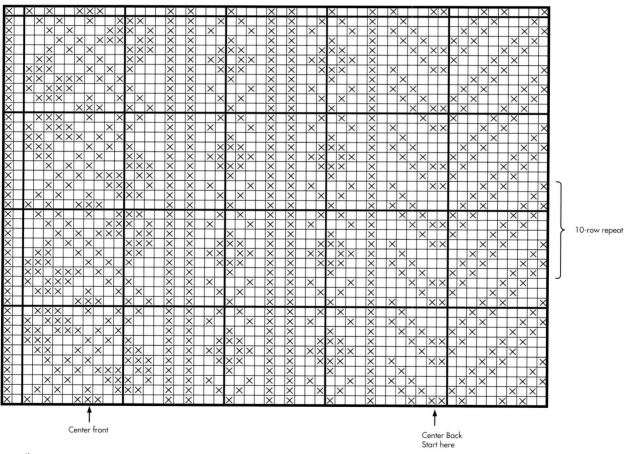

Center front

Center Back
Start here

10-row repeat

Chart A

Snuggle Socks

Sizes: S (M, L)

Finished Lengths: 13¾" (17", 19⅝") (35 cm (43 cm, 50 cm) long

Yarn: Fingering #1. *Shown here:* Sisu from Sandnes Garn (80% wool, 20% nylon)

Main Color (MC):   100 (100,150) grams of light blue no. 5930,
medium blue no. 5962, or dark blue no. 5575

Color A: 50 (50, 100) grams of white no. 1001

Alternative Yarn: Rauma Finullgarn (100% wool) – sky blue 472, dark navy blue 449,
deep navy blue 459, white 400

Needles: One set of five double pointed needles size US 3 (3.25 mm)

Gauge: 28 sts and 28 rows = 4" (10 cm) stockinette

CO 64 (72, 80) sts in MC and distribute evenly over 4 dpns. Join and k1, p1 for 2⅜" (2¾, 2¾)" (6 (7, 7) cm). On the next round, knit in stockinette, increasing by 5 sts evenly distributed across the round— sts 69 (77, 85). Knit pattern following the Knee-High Sock Chart for the size you are knitting (center back is the same for all sizes) until your work measures about 7⅛" (8⅝", 10¼")" (18 (22, 26) cm). Decrease 1 st at the beginning and the end of every 4th round at center back, until you have 48 (58, 62) sts. Continue to knit pattern until your work measures 13 (17, 19⅝)" (35 (43, 50) cm) or your desired length.

Heel: Make the heel using sts from the first and the fourth needle placed on to one needle, 24 (28, 30) sts total. Holding MC double, knit back and forth (knitting and purling) until you have a flap measuring 2 (2⅜, 2⅜)" 95 (6, 6) cm), then decrease to turn the heel: knit until you have 7 (8, 9) sts remaining on the left needle, turn, and purl until you have 7 (8, 9) sts remaining on the left needle, PM. You should now have 3 sections on your needles: 7 (8, 9) sts, 10 sts, 7 (8, 9) sts, with a marker in between each—24 sts. Turn, again, and knit until you have 1 st before the space. Sl1, k1, psso, turn, and purl until you have 1 st left before the space and p2tog. (Always leave the same number of sts on each side.) Continue decreasing in this manner on every row until you have 12 (14, 15) sts. Pick up 12 (14, 15) sts on each side of the heel, join with the top sts. Continue knitting in pattern across the instep, and knit the sole following Chart A. Knit until the foot measures about 6 (8, 8⅝")" (16 (20, 22) cm), or is at a desired length, before starting to decrease for the toe.

(The pattern is continued on page 14.)

Toe: Knit all sts following Chart A. Decrease for the toe at each side of the foot by knitting until you have 2 sts left on the first needle, sl1, k1, psso. K2tog at the beginning of the second needle. Knit until you have 2 sts remaining on the third needle, sl1, k1, psso. K2tog at the beginning of the fourth needle.

Continue decreasing on each round until you have 8 sts remaining. Cut the yarn and pull the it through the remaining sts. Weave in all loose ends.

Steam the socks carefully with an iron, and use a damp kitchen towel.

Knee-High Sock Chart M

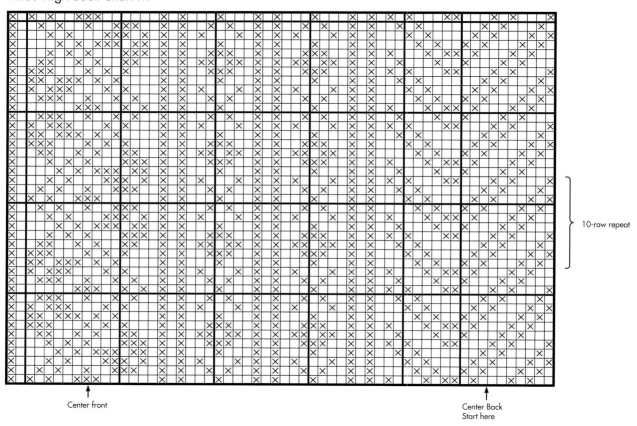

10-row repeat

Center front

Center Back
Start here

Chart A

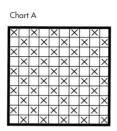

Knee-High Sock Chart L

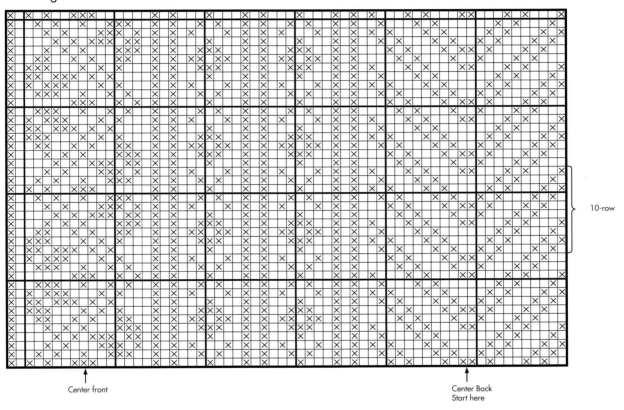

Center front

Center Back
Start here

10-row

Chart A

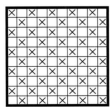

16" x 16"

Square Patterned Pillow

Finished Size: Approximately 16" x 16" (40 cm x 40 cm)

Yarn: Fingering #1. *Shown here:* Sisu from Sandnes Garn (80% wool, 20% nylon)

Main Color (MC): About 200 grams dark blue no. 5575, light blue no. 5930, or medium blue no. 5962

Color A: About 100 grams white no. 1001

Alternative Yarn: Rauma Finullgarn (100% wool) – sky blue 472, dark navy blue 449, deep navy blue 459, white 400

Needle: One 24" (60 cm) circular needle size US 10 (6 mm)

Gauge: 19 sts and 20 rows = 4" (10 cm) holding yarn double

Notions: 16" x 16" (40 cm x 40 cm) down pillow insert

Holding MC doubled, CO 160 sts. Pick up A, join, and knit 2 rounds. Following Square Patterned Pillow Chart, knit 6 10-row Drop 1 MC strand and pick up A. Following Pattern Chart, knit 6 10-row repeats and then finish as shown. Knit 2 rounds in MC. BO and weave in all loose ends.

Finishing: The pillow will look the best if you hand stitch the openings shut using double yarn. Doing this will also make it easy to open the seam when you want to wash the pillow cover. A down pillow insert will make the pillow especially soft and nice. Standard 16" x 16" (40 cm x 40 cm) down filled pillow inserts are easy to find at hobby shops and fabric stores.

Square Patterned Pillow Chart

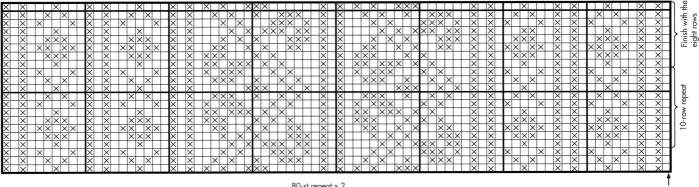

Finish with these eight rows

10-row repeat

80-st repeat x 2

Start here

The Cuddle Chair

Yarn: Fingering #1. *Shown here:* Sisu from Sandnes Garn (80% wool, 20% nylon)

Main Color (MC):   light blue no. 5930

Color A: white no. 1001

Alternative Yarn: Rauma Finullgarn (100% wool) – sky blue 472, white 400

Needle: One 16" (40 cm) circular needle size US 10 (6 mm)

Gauge: 19 sts and 20 rows = 4" (10 cm) double yarn

Notions: Chair, sewing machine, thread, a piece of cotton fabric large enough to back the finished knit piece, staple gun

Note: The cover for this chair is knit as "half" of the 16" x 24" (40 cm x 60 cm) Decorative Bed Pillow (page 22). All chairs are different, so make sure to measure your chair to get the right size for your cover before you begin.

Holding the MC doubled, CO 118 sts. Join and knit 2 rounds. Drop 1 strand of MC, pick up A, and knit the pattern following the chart on page 22 until you have the length you need. Finish as shown on the chart. Drop color A and pick up strand of MC. Holding MC doubled, knit 2 rounds in the main color. BO and weave in all loose ends.

Finishing: Using a sewing machine, sew 2 seams along the whole length of the piece at the second stitch at the beginning and 2 seams at the next to the last stitch. Cut the knit piece between these seams. Sew a zig-zag stitch over the raw edges. Slightly steam the piece. A knit piece is very stretchy, so you must mount it securely on a piece of cotton fabric before you use it on a piece of furniture. Any cotton fabric will work. It could be an old sheet, an old pillow case, or an ordinary piece of cotton.

Sew the cotton fabric and your knit piece together using a sewing machine. When your new cover is ready for use, attach it to the chair with a staple gun.

Decorative Bed Pillow

Finished Size: Approximately 16" x 24" (40 cm x 60 cm)

Yarn: Fingering #1. *Shown here:* Sisu from Sandnes Garn (80% wool, 20% nylon)

Main Color (MC):   About 300 grams light blue no. 5930

Color A: About 200 grams white 1001

Alternative Yarn: Rauma Finullgarn (100% wool) – sky blue 472, white 400

Needle: One 32" (80 cm) circular needle size US 10 (6 mm)

Gauge: 19 sts and 20 rows = 4" (10 cm) holding yarn double

Notions: 16"x24" (40 cm x 60 cm) down-filled pillow insert

Holding MC doubled, CO 236 sts. Join and knit 2 rounds. Drop 1 strand of MC and pick up A. Begin knitting following the Decorative Bed Pillow Chart. Knit 6 10-row repeats, and finish knitting following the chart. Drop A and pick up another strand of MC. Holding yarn double, knit 2 rounds. BO and weave in loose ends.

Finishing: The pillow will look the best if you close the openings by hand stitching with the yarn doubled. It will also make it easier to open the seam when you need to wash the cover. A down pillow insert will make the pillow especially nice and soft. Standard sized 16" x 24" (40 cm x 60 cm) pillow inserts. It is also possible to use a larger pillow insert measuring 20" x 26" (50 cm x 70 cm).

Decorative Bed Pillow Chart

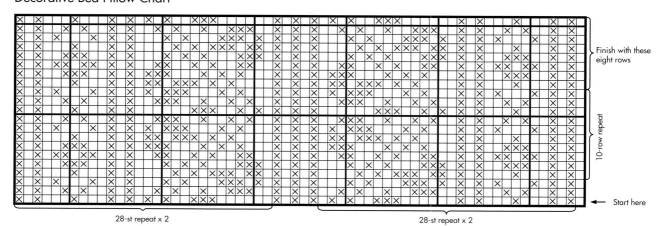

28-st repeat x 2   28-st repeat x 2

Finish with these eight rows

10-row repeat

← Start here

"I am always doing things I can't do, that's how I learn to do them ."

Pablo Picasso

What inspires me . . .

Roses

Laptop Cover

Size: This cover fits a 13" Mac (13" x 9"), you can adjust the size to fit your laptop.

Yarn: Fingering #1. *Shown here:* Sisu from Sandnes Garn (80% wool, 20% nylon)

Main Color (MC): 100 grams light pink no. 3911

Color A: 50 grams white no. 1001

Alternative Yarn: Rauma Finullgarn (100% wool) – lt pink 479, white 400

Needle: One 16" (40 cm) circular needle size US 3 (3.25 mm)

Gauge: 28 sts and 28 rows = 4" (10 cm) stockinette

Notions: One 18" (45 cm) long zipper, fabric for lining and batting for the inside of the cover (2 pieces of each, 13¾" x 9¾" (35 cm x 25 cm))

Note: The laptop cover is knit in two pieces. It could have been knit as one piece so you would only have to sew up the bottom and attach a zipper. However, all knits are very stretchy. Constructing this from two knit pieces stabilized with batting helps it hold its shape.

CO 156 sts in MC. Join and knit 2 rounds stockinette. On the next round, pick up A and begin knitting following the Laptop Cover Chart. Knit 8 10-row repeats until your piece measures about 14½" (37 cm). Finish knitting chart pattern as shown. Drop A and knit 2 rounds in MC. BO and weave in all loose ends. Repeat for the cover's back side.

Finishing: Using a sewing machine, sew 2, closely spaced seams along the second and fourth stitches on the MC column. Cut the piece along the middle of the third stitch. Press the cover pieces lightly using a damp kitchen towel. Cut the lining fabric and batting to the same size as your knit pieces. Place batting on the wrong side of the knitted piece and sew them together along the edges. Trim away excess material. Repeat for other panel. Place the knitted pieces on top of each other, right sides facing in, and sew along the sides and the bottom, making slightly rounded corners.

To attach the zipper, turn the cover inside out, fold in the top edges, and sew the zipper in using a sewing machine, rounding the corners as you go.

Place the lining pieces on top of each other right side facing in, and sew the bottom and sides together. Round the corners slightly at the bottom and the top of the lining where the zipper goes. Put the lining into the knit cover and attach it by hand stitching using invisible stitches.

Laptop Cover Chart

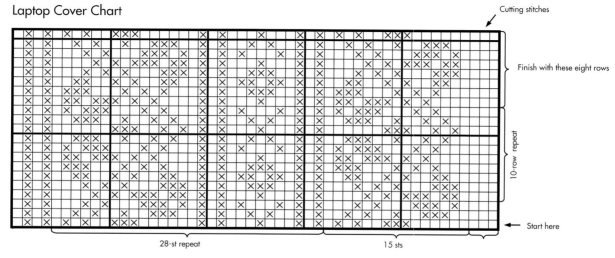

28

Snuggle Throw

Finished Size: 45¼" x 88⅝" (115 cm x 225 cm)

Yarn: Fingering #1. *Shown here:* Sisu from Sandnes Garn (80% wool, 20% nylon)

Color A: 200 grams light pink no. 3911

Color B: 200 grams white no. 1001

Color C: 250 grams medium pink no. 4517

Color D: 700 grams dark pink no. 4627

Alternative Yarn: Rauma Finullgarn (100% wool) – lt pink 479, med rose 465, dk rose 456, white 400

Crochet Hook: C-2 (2.75 mm) or D-3 (3.25 mm)

Note: This throw is made up of 180 granny squares, 10 squares wide and 18 squares long. You can decide how many colors and which colors you want to use.

INSTRUCTIONS FOR CROCHETING A GRANNY SQUARE:

Chain (ch) 4 stitches and slip stitch (sl st) into the first stitch (st) to form a ring.

Round 1 (Color A): Ch 3, 2 dc into the ring * ch 2, 3 dc into the same ring*. Repeat * - * 2 times. Ch 2. Attach the last ch with 1 sl st into the top of the ch 3, 2 sl sts to ch corner space. You have now made a small square with 4 corners.

Round 2 (Color A): Ch 3, 2 dc, ch 2, 3 dc into ch corner space * ch 1, 3 dc, ch 2, 3 dc into the next ch corner space *. Repeat * - * 2 more times. Ch 1. Attach the last ch with 1 sl st into the top of the ch 3, and 2 sl sts to the ch corner space. Cut the yarn and pull the thread all the way through.

Round 3 (Color B): Change yarn color and attach at a corner space. Ch 3, 2 dc, ch 2, 3 dc into ch corner space. Crochet * ch 1, 3 dc into next ch space, ch 1, 3 dc, ch 2, 3 dc in the next ch corner space *. Repeat * - * 2 more times. Ch 1, 3 dc into ch space, ch 1. Attach the last ch with 1 sl st into the top of the ch 3, and crochet 2 sl sts to the ch corner space. Cut the yarn and pull it completely through.

Round 4 (Color C): Change yarn color and attach at a corner space. Ch 3, 2 dc, ch 2, 3 dc into the ch corner space. Crochet * ch 1, 3 dc, ch 1 into each of the next 2 ch spaces. 3 dc, ch 2, 3 dc into the next ch corner space * . Repeat * - * 2 more times.

Ch 1, 3 dc, ch 1 into each of the next 2 ch spaces. Attach the last ch with 1 sl st into the top of the ch 3, and crochet 2 sl sts to the ch corner space. Cut the yarn and pull it completely through.

Round 5 (Color D): Change yarn color and attach at a corner space. Ch 3, 2 dc, ch 2, 3 dc into ch corner space. Crochet * ch 1, 3 dc, ch 1 into each of the next 3 ch spaces. 3 dc, ch 2, 3 dc in the next ch corner space * . Repeat * - * 2 more times. Ch 1, 3 dc, ch 1 into each of the next 3 ch spaces. Attach the last ch with 1 sl st into the top of the ch 3, and crochet 2 sl sts to the ch corner space, but do not cut the yarn.

Round 6 (Color D): Ch 3, 2 dc, ch 2, 3 dc in ch corner space. Crochet * ch 1, 3 dc, ch 1 into each of the next 4 ch spaces. 3 dc, ch 2, 3 dc into the next ch corner space * . Repeat * – * 2 more times. Ch 1, 3 dc, ch 1 into each of the next 4 ch spaces. Attach the last ch with 1 sl st into the top of the ch 3, and crochet 2 sl sts to the ch corner space. Cut the yarn and pull it completely through.

Finishing: Weave in all loose ends and sew or crochet the squares together using whatever method you prefer. Finish the throw by crocheting a border around the entire throw using 3 dc, ch 1 into each ch space, and 3 dc, ch 2, 3 dc into each ch corner space. Repeat, 2 or 3 more rounds.

ONE PILLOW, One Color

Finished Size: Approximately 20" x 20" (50 cm)

Yarn: Fingering #1. *Shown here:* Sisu from Sandnes Garn (80% wool, 20% nylon)

Main Color (MC):   About 200 grams dark pink no. 4627

Alternative Yarn: Rauma Finullgarn (100% wool) – dk rose 456

Needles: One 24" circular needle US 10 (6 mm)

Gauge: 17 sts and 20 rows = 4" (10 cm) stockinette with yarn held double

Notions: 20" x 20" (50 cm x 50 cm) pillow insert

Note: A cozy pillow knit in a single color complements patterned knit pillows very well. You may want to knit your solid colored pillow in the same main color as your patterned pillow, as shown here, to create a cohesive look.

Holding the yarn double, CO 160 sts. Join and knit in the round until your pillow is 20" (50 cm) long. BO and weave in all loose ends.

Finishing: The pillow will look best if you hand sew the openings together using double yarn. This makes it easier to remove the seam and take out remove the pillow when you want to launder the cover. A down filled insert will make the pillow especially soft and nice. Down inserts in the given dimensions are easy to find at hobby and craft stores.

BABY
Blanket

Finished Size: Approximately 29½" x 33½" (75 cm x 85 cm)

Yarn: Fingering #1. *Shown here:* Sisu from Sandnes Garn (80% wool, 20% nylon)

Main Color (MC): About 300 grams light pink no. 3911

Color A: About 150 grams white no. 1001

Alternative Yarn: Rauma Finullgarn (100% wool) – lt pink 479, white 400

Needles: One 32" (80 cm) circular needle size US 3 (3.25 mm); Two double-pointed or one set of straight - needles size US 3 (3.25 mm)

Gauge: 28 sts and 28 rows = 4" (10 cm) stockinette

Notions: ¼" (0.5 cm) wide silk ribbon, sewing machine, thread

Using the circular needles, CO 213 sts in MC. Join and knit 2 rounds. On the next round, k2 in MC, knit 7 28-st repeats of the chart, k2 in MC. Continue in this manner, knitting 21 10-row repeats of the chart for the length. Finish according to the chart and knit 2 rounds in MC. BO and weave in all loose ends.

Finishing: Using a sewing machine, sew 2, closely spaced seams along the second and fourth stitches on the MC column. Cut the piece along the middle of the third stitch. Use the sewing machine to sew a zig zag seam over both raw edges.

Edging: Using the double-pointed or straight needles, CO 15 sts in the main color. Knit an approximately 4 yards (3.6 meters) long stockinette band. Measure your edging band as you knit to make sure that it is long enough for your blanket. BO.

Your blanket will hold its shape nicely if you sew a narrow ribbon along all the edges before attaching the edging band. I used a ¼" (0.5 cm) wide silk ribbon. Measure the blanket to determined how long your ribbon needs to be. Use a sewing machine to attach the ribbon to the blanket. Place the purled side of the knit edging on top of the blanket's right (patterned) side, and stitch it in place along the edges using a sewing machine. Fold the edging over and attach it to the wrong side of the blanket by hand stitching.

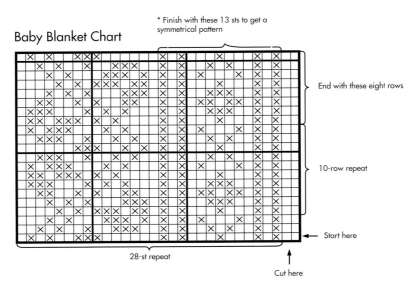

Baby Blanket Chart

* Finish with these 13 sts to get a symmetrical pattern

End with these eight rows

10-row repeat

Start here

28-st repeat

Cut here

Sleeves for Glass Jars

Finished Size: 4⅜" (5½") (11 (14 cm))
Yarn: Fingering #1. *Shown here:* Sisu from Sandnes Garn (80% wool, 20% nylon)
Main Color (MC): 50 grams light pink no. 3911 (medium pink no. 4517)
Color A: 50 grams white no. 1001
Alternative Yarn: Rauma Finullgarn (100% wool) – lt pink 479, med rose 465, white 400
Needles: One set of five double-pointed needles size US 3 (3.25 mm) (US 4 (3.5 mm))
Gauge: 28 sts and 28 rows = 4" (10 cm) stockinette
Notions: 1 quart (1 liter) (1 pint (½ liter)) glass canning jars

CO 76 sts in MC and distribute evenly over 3or 4 dpns join and knit about 2¼" (5.5 cm) (2¾" (7 cm)) in stockinette. Purl 1 round and knit 1 round. On the next round pick up A and begin following the Glass Jar Sleeves Chart. Knit 2 (3) 10-row repeats, and finish as shown on the chart. Knit 1 round and purl 1 round in MC. Continue knitting in stockinette in MC for about 2¾" (7 cm) (2¼" (5.5 cm).

BO and weave in all loose ends. Fold the edges in the main color towards the inside of the cover and sew them in place on the purl side. The cover will then be double layered and should fit perfectly over a 1 quart (liter) (1 pint (½ liter)) glass canning jar. Do not steam press the cover, because doing this will make the knitting expand and become too big for the jar.

Glass Jar Sleeves Chart

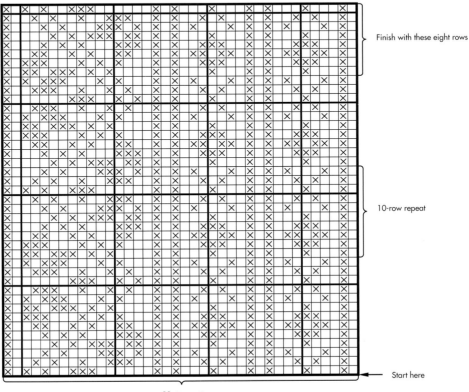

Finish with these eight rows

10-row repeat

Start here

38-st repeat

TWIN BED
Blanket

Finished Size: Approximately 41¼" x 71" (105 cm x 180 cm)

Yarn: Fingering #1. *Shown here:* Sisu from Sandnes Garn (80% wool, 20% nylon)

Main Color (MC): About 650 grams light pink no. 3911

Color A: About 400 grams white no. 1001 or dark pink no. 4627

Alternative Yarn: Rauma Finullgarn (100% wool) – white 400 and lt pink 479 or dk rose 456

Needles: One 32" (80 cm) circular needle size US 3 (3.25 mm) and two double-pointed or one set of straight needles size US 3 (3.25 mm)

Gauge: 28 sts and 28 rows = 4" (10 cm)

Notions: Sewing machine; thread; ¼" (0.5 cm) wide silk ribbon, approx. 6⅕ yards (6 meters) long

Using MC and circular needle, CO 297 sts. Join and knit 2 rounds. On the next round, k 2 in MC, pick up A and knit 10 28-st repeats of the Twin Bed Blanket Chart, k2 in MC. Continue in this manner, knitting 44 10-row repeats of the chart for the length. Finish off the blanket according to the chart, and then knit 2 rounds in MC. BO and weave in all loose ends.

Finishing: Using a sewing machine, sew 2, closely spaced seams along the second and fourth stitches on the MC column. Cut the blanket along the middle of the third stitch. Use the sewing machine to sew a zig zag seam over both raw edges.

Edging: Using the MC and straight or double-pointed needles, CO 20 sts. Knit back and forth in stockinette until you have an edging band measuring

about 6½ yards (6 meters). Remember to measure your blanket to make sure that your edging band is long enough. BO and weave in all loose ends.

Attaching the edging: Your blanket will hold its shape nicely if you sew a narrow ribbon along all the edges before attaching the edging band. A ¼" (0.5 cm) wide silk ribbon will work well. Measure your blanket to determine how long your ribbon should be. Sew it on along all the blanket's edges using a sewing machine. Next, place the purled side of the knit edging on top of the edge of the blanket's right (patterned) side, and sew it onto the blanket using a sewing machine. Fold the edging band over and attach it to the wrong side of the blanket by hand stitching.

Twin Bed Blanket Chart

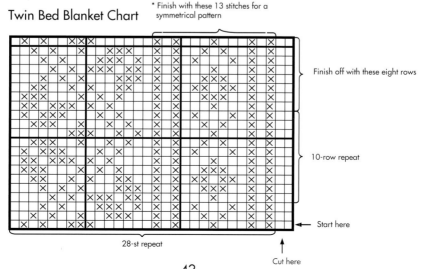

* Finish with these 13 stitches for a symmetrical pattern

Finish off with these eight rows

10-row repeat

Start here

28-st repeat

Cut here

SHORT
Snuggle Socks

Size: One Size
Yarn: Fingering #1. *Shown here:* Sisu from Sandnes Garn (80% wool, 20% nylon)
Main Color (MC): (100 grams) light pink no. 3911
Color A: 50 grams white no. 1001
Alternative Yarn: Rauma Finullgarn (100% wool) – lt pink 479, white 400
Needles: One set five double-pointed needles size US 3 (3.25 mm)
Gauge: 28 sts and 28 rows = 4" (10 cm) stockinette
Note: The ribbing on this sock makes it very elastic, so it will fit an adult or a child's foot equally well. All you have to do is adjust the length.

Using MC and double-pointed needles, CO 60 sts on and distribute evenly across 4 needles. Join and k1, p1 for 3 rounds. On the next round pick up A and begin knitting the pattern according to the Short Snuggle Socks Chart. Knit 2 rounds in MC only. Knit the next round as follows: * Knit sts together, yo *. Repeat * – * across the round. Knit another 4 rounds. Turn your work inside out, so that the purl side is on the outside. On the next round, k2, p2 until your work measures about 8" – 10" (20 – 25 cm), or until you have the length you want, before starting on the heel.

Heel: Place the sts from the 1st and the 4th needles on 1 needle 30 sts total. You may choose to hold the yarn doubled for a sturdier heel. Knit back and forth (knit a row, purl a row) until you have a flap measuring 2⅜" (6 cm) then decrease as follows: knit until you have 9 sts remaining on the left needle, turn

and purl until you have 9 sts remaining on the left needle. You should now have 3 sections on your needles: 9 sts, 12 sts, 9 sts, with a space in between each — 30 sts total. Turn and knit until you have 1 st before the space, sl1, k1, psso to right needle. Turn and purl until you have 1 st left before the space and 2 tog across the space. (Always leave the same number of sts on each side.) Continue decreasing in this until you reach the end of each row.

Foot: Pick up 15 sts along the side of the heel flap, k2, p2 across the instep stitches, pick up 15 stitches along the other side of the heel flap, knit across the remaining heel stitches. Join and proceed knitting in the round (k2, p2 for the instep stitches, knit only for the sole stitches).

(The pattern is continued on page 47.)

Short Snuggle Socks Chart

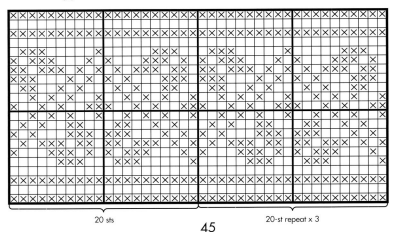

20 sts   20-st repeat x 3

Toe: Knit until you have 2 sts left on the first needle, sl1, k1, psso. K2tog on the second needle. Knit until you have 2 sts left on the third needle, sl1, k1, psso. K2tog on the fourth needle. Continue to decrease in this way until you have 8 sts left. Cut the yarn and pull it through the remaining sts. Weave in all loose ends.

Finishing: Steam the socks carefully using a damp kitchen towel. Fold the cuff so that the picot edging shows.

What inspires me . . .

Stone Walls

TWIN BED
Blanket

Finished Size: About 41¼" x 71" (105 cm x 180 cm)
Yarn: Fingering #1. *Shown here:* Sisu from Sandnes Garn (80% wool, 20% nylon)
Main Color (MC): About 650 grams light gray no. 1042
Color A: About 400 grams white no. 1001
Alternative Yarn: Rauma Finullgarn (100% wool) – dk gray heather 405, white 400
Needles: One 32" (80 cm) circular needle size US 3 (3.25 mm);
     One set of straight or two double-pointed needles size US 3 (3.25 mm)
Gauge: 28 sts and 28 rows = 4" (10 cm) in pattern
Notions: Sewing machine, thread, approx. 6½ yards ¼" wide silk ribbon

CO 297 sts in MC. Join and knit 2 rounds. On the next round, k 2 in MC, k 10 repeats of the chart (ending with the first part of the pattern repeat market by an *), k 2 in MC. Continue in this manner, knitting 44 repeats of the chart for the length. Finish off the blanket according to the chart, and knit 2 rounds in MC. BO and weave in all loose ends.

Finishing: You will cut open the knit piece in the column of 4 sts in MC. Using a sewing machine, sew two, closely spaced seams along the second and fourth stitches on the MC column. Cut the along the middle of the third stitch. Use the sewing machine to sew a zig zag seam over both raw edges.

Edging: Using MC, CO 20 sts on a straight or double-pointed needle. Knit back and forth in

stockinette stitch (knit a row, purl a row) until you have an edging band measuring about 6½ yards (6 meters). Remember to measure your blanket to make sure that the edging band is long enough. BO and weave in loose ends.

Attaching the edging band: To stabilize the blanket edges, first sew a ¼" (0.5 cm) wide silk ribbon along all the edges before attaching the edging band. Measure your blanket to get the right length for the ribbon. Sew it on along all the blanket's edges using a sewing machine. Next, place the purled side of the knit edging on top of the blanket's right (patterned) side, and stitch it in place along the edges using a sewing machine. Fold the edging over and attach it to the wrong side of the blanket by hand stitching.

Twin Bed Blanket Chart

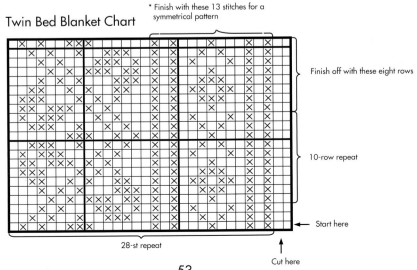

We live in a time that is sadly dominated by vast consumerism. My response to this has been to shift my focus from always having new things to finding ways to repurpose what I already have. Knitting or crocheting a beautiful throw requires a lot of time and patience. Why not find another use for it as a tablecloth for special occasions? A stunning table setting, delicious food, and good conversation all contribute to a memorable evening.

COVER FOR A
Stool

Finished Size: Approximately 16" x 16" (40 cm x 40 cm)

Yarn: Fingering #1. *Shown here:* Sisu from Sandnes Garn (80% wool, 20% nylon)

Main Color (MC): 100 grams light gray no. 1042 or Black no. 1099

Color A: white no. 1001

Alternative Yarn: Rauma Finullgarn (100% wool) – dk gray heather 405, black 436, white 400.

Needle: One 16" (40 cm) circular needle size US 3 (3.25 mm)

Gauge: 28 sts and 28 rows = 4" (10 cm) stockinette

Notions: Sewing machine, thread, cotton cloth, stool, staple gun

Using MC, CO 116 sts. Join and knit 2 rounds. On the next round, k2 in MC, pick up A, and knit following chart for 4 28-st repeats, k2 in MC—112 sts. Continue knitting for 10 10-row repeats of the chart or until the piece measures about 16" (40 cm). Finish off according to the chart. Knit 2 rounds in MC. BO and weave in all loose ends.

Finishing: Using a sewing machine, sew 2, closely spaced seams along the second and fourth stitches on the MC column. Cut the along the middle of the third stitch. Use the sewing machine to sew a zig zag seam over both raw edges. Slightly steam your piece. A knit piece is very stretchy, so to use it on a piece of furniture you must mount it on a piece of cotton to stabilize its shape. Any piece of cotton will do, such as an old pillow case or comforter cover, or a regular piece of cotton.

Place the fabric on the wrong side of the knit piece and use a sewing machine to stitch the 2 together along all the edges. Next, fasten the knit cover to the bottom of the stool's seat using a staple gun.

Stool Cover Chart

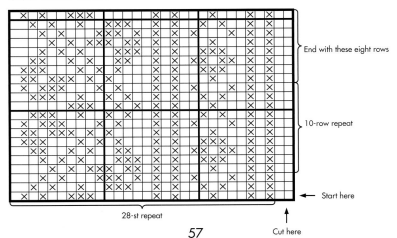

End with these eight rows

10-row repeat

Start here

28-st repeat

Cut here

Storage Bag

Finished Size: Approximately 16½" x 13¾" (42 cm x 35 cm)
Yarn: Fingering #1. *Shown here:* Sisu from Sandnes Garn (80% wool, 20% nylon)
Main Color (MC):   150 grams black no. 1099 or light gray no. 1042
Color A: 100 grams white no. 1001
Alternative Yarn: Rauma Finullgarn (100% wool) – dk gray heather 405, black 436, white 400
Needle: One 32" (80 cm) circular needle size US 3 (3.25 mm), 32" (80 cm) long
Gauge: 28 sts and 28 rows = 4" (10 cm) stockinette
Notions: Fabric, sewing machine, thread

Using MC, CO 196 sts. Join and knit 2 rounds. On the next round pick up A and begin following the chart as follows: * Knit the 28-st repeat 3 times, and then knit the 14-st repeat twice *. You are now halfway through the round. Knit *-* once again. Continue in this manner until you have completed 10 10-row repeats for the length. Next, knit the last 8 rounds according to the chart. Divide your work into 2 equal parts, a front side and a back side, 98 sts each. Using MC, knit the front and back sides separately in stockinette (knit a row, purl a row) for about 2½" (6 cm). BO and weave in all loose ends. The MC section at the top edge of the bag will be folded under to create a pocket for the drawstring.

Lining: Line the knit bag with a bag made from fabric. You can use any fabric you already own, such as an old pillow case, comforter cover, or anything similar. Or, you may simply choose an ordinary cotton textile.

Cut 2 pieces of fabric to the same size as 1 side of the knit bag. Place the 2 pieces of fabric on top of each other, right sides facing, and use a sewing machine to sew the pieces together along 3 sides. Place the fabric bag inside the knit bag. Fold the knit top edge over the raw fabric edge on 1 side, and use a sewing machine to attach the pieces. Do the same on the other side. Twist yarn together to make a drawstring. Thread the drawstring through the pocket created by the folded over knit piece and tie the ends together to create the bag's strap.

Storage Bag Chart

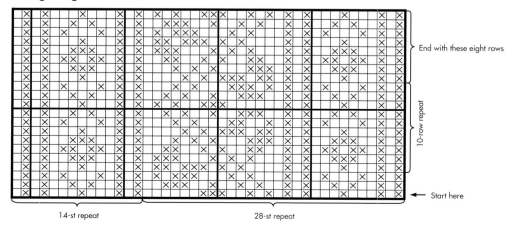

End with these eight rows

10-row repeat

Start here

14-st repeat

28-st repeat

Single Yarn Chair Cover

Finished Size: Approximately 21¼" x 23¾" (54 cm x 60 cm)

Yarn: Fingering #1. *Shown here:* Sisu from Sandnes Garn (80% wool, 20% nylon)

Main Color (MC): 100 grams black no. 1099

Color A: 100 grams white no. 1001

Alternative Yarn: Rauma Finullgarn (100% wool) – black 436, white 400

Needle: One 24" (60 cm) circular needle size US 3 (3.25 mm), 24" (60 cm) long

Gauge: 28 sts and 28 rows = 4" (10 cm) stockinette

Notions: Chair, sewing machine, thread, fabric, staple gun

Note: All chairs are different. Be sure to measure your chair's seat to determine the dimensions needed for your cover. You may need to adjust the amount of stitches and repeats necessary to achieve these dimensions.

Using MC, CO 172 sts. Join and knit 2 rounds. On the next round, k2 in MC, pick up A, and follow the Stool Cover Chart on page 57 for 6 28-st repeats, k2 st in MC — 168 sts. Starting and ending each round with 2 sts in MC leaves a space for cutting open your work.

Continue knitting until your piece is of the right length for your chair's seat. The pictured chair seat needed 13 10-row repeats and the last rounds were knit according to the chart. Knit the last 2 rounds in MC. BO and weave in all loose ends.

Finishing: Using a sewing machine, sew 2, closely spaced seams along the second and fourth stitches on the MC column. Cut the along the middle of the third stitch. Use the sewing machine to sew a zig zag seam over both raw edges. Lightly steam your piece. All knits are very stretchy, so you must stabilize your knit seat cover by sewing it to a piece of cotton fabric. Use any fabric you have at hand, an old pillow case, a comforter cover, or an ordinary piece of cotton fabric.

Sew the knit and fabric edges together using a sewing machine. Then place the cover on the seat and staple the edges underneath with a staple gun.

The pictured chair was painted in a black color with a satin finish.

Double Yarn Chair Cover

Finished Size: Approximately 23¼" x 23¾" (59 cm x 60 cm)

Yarn: Fingering #1. *Shown here:* Sisu from Sandnes Garn (80% wool, 20% nylon)

Main Color (MC):   About 200 grams light gray no. 1042

Color A: About 200 grams white no. 1001

Alternative Yarn: Rauma Finullgarn (100% wool) – dk gray heather 405, white 400

Needle: One 16" (40 cm) circular needle size US 10 (6 mm)

Gauge: 19 sts and 20 rows = 4" (10 cm) stockinette with yarn doubled

Notions: Chair, sewing machine, thread, fabric, staple gun

Note: All chairs are different. Be sure to measure your chair's seat to determine the dimensions needed for your cover. You may need to adjust the amount of stitches and repeats necessary to achieve these dimensions.

Using MC held double, CO 118 sts. Join and knit 2 rounds. On the next round, pick up 2 strands of A and knit the pattern following the Decorative Bed Pillow Chart on page 22. We completed 8 10-row repeats for this cover, but you may need more or less depending on the dimensions of your seat. Finish knitting your cover according to the chart, and then knit 2 rounds in MC. BO and weave in all loose ends.

Finishing: Using a sewing machine, sew 2 closely spaced seams along the second stitches at the beginning of your seat cover, and 2 closely spaced seams along the next to the last stitches. Cut open your knit seat cover between these 2 pairs of seams.

Sew zig zag seams over the raw edges. Lightly steam the piece. All knits are very stretchy , so you must stabilize your knit cover by sewing it onto a piece of cotton fabric. Use any fabric you have at hand, an old pillow case, a comforter cover, or an ordinary piece of cotton fabric.

Use a sewing machine to sew the knit seat cover and fabric edges together. Then place the cover on the seat and staple the edges underneath with a staple gun.

The pictured chair was painted in a "soft" black color with a satin finish.

16" x 24"

ONE PILLOW,
One Color

Finished Size: Approximately 16" x 24" (40 cm x 60 cm)
Yarn: Fingering #1. *Shown here:* Sisu from Sandnes Garn (80% wool, 20% nylon)
Main Color (MC): About 300 grams dark gray no. 1088
Alternative Yarn: Rauma Finullgarn (100% wool) – charcoal gray heather 414
Needle: One 32" (80 cm) circular needle US 10 (6 mm)
Gauge: 17 sts and 20 rows = 4" (10 cm) stockinette with yarn doubled
Notions: Down pillow insert 16" x 24" (40 cm x 60 cm)
Note: A solid-colored pillow will work well with any patterned pillow, especially if the color of the solid-colored pillow matches the main color of the patterned pillow.

Holding the yarn double, CO 160 sts. Join and knit in the round until your pillow is 20" (50 cm) long. BO and weave in all loose ends.

Finishing: The pillow will look best if you hand sew the openings together using double yarn. This makes it easier to remove the seam and take out remove the pillow when you want to launder the cover. A down filled insert will make the pillow especially soft and nice. Down inserts in the given dimensions are easy to find at hobby and craft stores.

iPhone Sock

Finished Size: The Sock fits an iPhone 4. Adjust gauge and/or pattern repeats as needed to fit another phone type.

Yarn: Fingering #1. *Shown here:* Sisu from Sandnes Garn (80% wool, 20% nylon)

Main Color (MC):   50 grams moss green no. 9072

Color A: 50 grams white no. 1001

Alternative Yarn: Rauma Finullgarn (100% wool) – dk green 432, white 400

Needles: One set of five double-pointed needles size US 3 (3.25 mm)

Gauge: 28 sts and 28 rows = 4" (10 cm) stockinette

Notions: Button or snap

Using MC, CO 84 sts and distribute evenly over 4 dpns. Join, pick up A, and knit 2 rounds stockinette. Pick up A and begin following the iPhone Sock Chart, completing 2 42-st repeats — 84sts. Knit for two 10-row repeats, or until your work measures about 4½" (11 cm). Knit the 8 finishing rows according to the chart. Knit 1 round and purl 1 round in MC. Knit 3 rounds in MC. BO and weave in all loose ends.

Finishing: Fold over the top o the purled ridge creates a nice edge, and sew the flap down inside the sock. Sew the sock's bottom end shut with yarn.

Tab: Using MC, CO on 15 sts and knit a ⅝" (1.5 cm) long strip in stockinette. BO weave in all loose ends, and attach the tab to the sock in the middle of the back side. Attach a button or snap button to close the tab at the front of the sock.

You can make a string for hanging the iPhone sock around your neck, if you want to carry the case this way. Simply twist several strings of yarn together, knot the ends, and attach the ends to the sides of the phone case.

iPhone Sock Chart

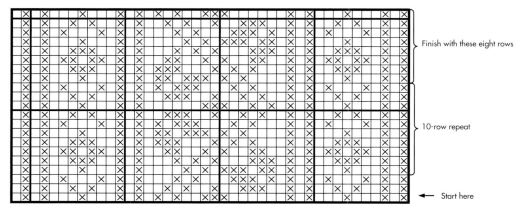

Finish with these eight rows

10-row repeat

← Start here

42-st repeat

SHORT Snuggle Socks

Finished Size: One Size
Yarn: Fingering #1. *Shown here:* Sisu from Sandnes Garn (80% wool, 20% nylon)
Main Color (MC): 100 grams light gray no. 1042
Color A: 50 grams white no. 1001
Alternative Yarn: Rauma Finullgarn (100% wool) – dk gray heather 405; white 400
Needles: One set of five double-pointed needles size US 3 (3.25 mm) or size needed to obtain gauge
Gauge: 28 sts and 28 rows = 4" (10 cm) stockinette
Note: The ribbing on this sock makes it very elastic, so it will fit an adult or a child's foot equally well. All you have to do is adjust the length.

Using MC and double-pointed needles, CO 60 sts on and distribute evenly across 4 needles. Join and k1, p1 for 3 rounds. On the next round pick up A and begin knitting the pattern according to the Short Snuggle Socks Chart. Knit 2 rounds in MC only. Knit the next round as follows: * Knit sts together, yo *. Repeat * – * across the round. Knit another 4 rounds. Turn your work inside out, so that the purl side is on the outside. On the next round, k2, p2 until your work measures about 8" – 10" (20 – 25 cm), or until you have the length you want, before starting on the heel.

Heel: Place the sts from the 1st and the 4th needles on 1 needle 30 sts total. You may choose to hold the yarn doubled for a sturdier heel. Knit back and forth (knit a row, purl a row) until you have a flap measuring 2⅜" (6 cm) then decrease as follows: knit until you have 9 sts remaining on the left needle, turn and purl until you have 9 sts remaining on the left needle. You should now have 3 sections on your needles: 9 sts, 12 sts, 9 sts, with a space in between each — 30 sts total. Turn and knit until you have 1 st before the space, sl1, k1, psso to right needle. Turn and purl until you have 1 st left before the space and 2 tog across the space. (Always leave the same number of sts on each side.) Continue decreasing in this until you reach the end of each row.

(The pattern is continued on page 71.)

Short Snuggle Socks Chart

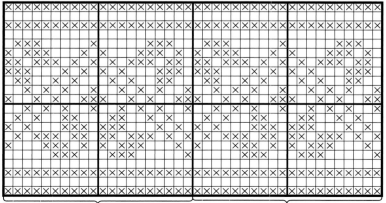

20 sts   20 sts x 3

Foot: Pick up 15 sts along the side of the heel flap, k2, p2 across the instep stitches, pick up 15 stitches along the other side of the heel flap, knit across the remaining heel stitches. Join and proceed knitting in the round (k2, p2 for the instep stitches, knit only for the sole stitches).

Toe: Knit until you have 2 sts left on the first needle, sl1, k1, psso. K2tog on the second needle. Knit until you have 2 sts left on the third needle, sl1, k1, psso. K2tog on the fourth needle. Continue to decrease in this way until you have 8 sts left. Cut the yarn and pull it through the remaining sts. Weave in all loose ends.

Finishing: Steam the socks carefully using a damp kitchen towel. Fold the cuff so that the picot edging shows.

Cozy Sweater

Sizes: S/M (L/XL)

Finished measurements: Chest width 39½ (45)" (100 (114) cm) **Total Length** 27 (28½)" (69 (72) cm)

Yarn: Chunky #5. *Shown here:* Fritidsgarn from Sandnes Garn (100% wool)

Main Color (MC): 450 (500) grams dark gray no. 1055 or light gray no. 1042

Color A: 50 grams white no. 1012

Alternative Yarn: Aran #4. Rauma Vamsegarn (100% wool) – charcoal gray heather V14, or gray heather V13, white V00

Needles: One 32" (80 cm) circular needle; One set of five double-pointed needles size US 10 (6 mm); One crochet hook size US J -10 (6 mm)

Gauge: 15 sts and 18 rows = 4" (10 cm) stockinette

Notions: Stitch markers

Body: Using MC, CO 140 (160) sts. Join and knit 10 rounds stockinette. On the next round, pick up A and continue knitting following the Cozy Sweater Chart. Start the pattern at the arrow for the size you have chosen. After you have completed the chart, place a stitch marker at the beginning of the next round. Using MC, knit 70 (80) sts, place another marker, and finish the round. Continue knitting until the body measures about 17¾ (18¼)" (45 (46) cm). On the next round, knit until you have 3 sts left before the side stitch marker, BO 7 sts. Continue knitting until you have 3 sts before the next stitch marker, BO 7 sts. Set the body aside.

Sleeves: Using MC, CO 36 (38) sts and distribute evenly across 4 dpns. Join, place a stitch marker, and knit stockinette until your work measures 2" (5 cm). On the next round, increase 1 st on each side of the stitch marker = 38 (40) sts total. Continue in stockinette and increase 2 sts about every 2" (5 cm) until you have 54 (56) sts total. Continue knitting until the sleeve measures about 19¾ (20½)" (50 (52) cm). Set the sleeve aside and repeat the process for the second sleeve.

Raglan Decrease: Transfer the sleeves to the circular needle with the body, lining up the bound-off stitches on either side of the body with the bound-off stitches on the sleeves. You should have 220 (244) sts total on the needle. Knit one round, placing a stitch marker at each place a sleeve joins to the body—

4 stitch markers. Start the raglan decrease on the next round. Knit until you have 4 sts left before the first stitch marker, sl1, k1, psso, k4, k2tog. Repeat these decreases at each stitch marker in this round. Continue to knit and repeat the raglan decreases at every other round, a total of 15 (16) times. Your sweater should measure about 25¼ (26)" (64 (66) cm). Now make decreases for the neck opening while continuing the raglan decreases.

Neck Opening: BO 11 (13) sts at the sweater's front center. Knit back and forth in stockinette, still performing raglan decreases as before. Decrease by binding off stitches on each side of the neck opening every other row as follows: 2 sts, 2 sts, 1 st, 1 st, 1 st — 35 (41) sts remain; 20 (22) raglan decreases completed. BO all stitches and weave in all loose ends. Sew shut the openings under the arms. Lightly steam the sweater.

Finish off by crocheting a row of slip sts around the neck opening using a crochet hook.

Cozy Sweater Chart

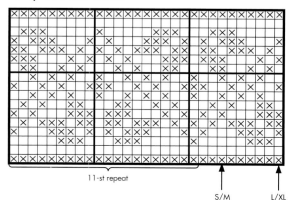

11-st repeat

S/M   L/XL

In my experience, one of the best things
in life is to take a hike in the high
mountains; it doesn't matter the season.
What does matter is the satisfying sense
of accomplishment at reaching my goal.
Afterward, the body is tired but content,
and a warm shower is welcome. I delight
in slipping on cozy wool socks and a
delicious, warm and comfortable sweater.
What could be better?

What inspires me . . .

Nature

Crochet Throw

Finished size: Approximately 45¼" x 88⅝" (115 cm x 225 cm)

Yarn: Fingering #1. *Shown here:* Sisu from Sandnes Garn (80% wool, 20% nylon)

Color A: 200 grams Beige no. 3021

Color B: 200 grams White no. 1001

Color C: 250 grams Light Brown no. 3161

Color D: 700 grams Dark Brown no. 3082

Alternative Yarn: Rauma Finullgarn (100% wool) – bone 452, white 400, med brown heather 411, dk brown 422

Crochet Hook: (3 mm)

INSTRUCTIONS FOR CROCHETING A GRANNY SQUARE:

Chain (ch) 4 stitches and slip stitch (sl st) into the first stitch (st) to form a ring.

Round 1 (Color A): Ch 3, 2 dc into the ring * ch 2, 3 dc into the same ring*. Repeat * - * 2 times. Ch 2. Attach the last ch with 1 sl st into the top of the ch 3, 2 sl sts to ch corner space. You have now made a small square with 4 corners.

Round 2 (Color A): Ch 3, 2 dc, ch 2, 3 dc into ch corner space * ch 1, 3 dc, ch 2, 3 dc into the next ch corner space *. Repeat * - * 2 more times. Ch 1. Attach the last ch with 1 sl st into the top of the ch 3, and 2 sl sts to the ch corner space . Cut the yarn and pull the thread all the way through.

Round 3 (Color B): Change yarn color and attach at a corner space. Ch 3, 2 dc, ch 2, 3 dc into ch corner space. Crochet * ch 1, 3 dc into next ch space, ch 1, 3 dc, ch 2, 3 dc in the next ch corner space *. Repeat * - * 2 more times. Ch 1, 3 dc into ch space, ch 1. Attach the last ch with 1 sl st into the top of the ch 3, and crochet 2 sl sts to the ch corner space. Cut the yarn and pull it completely through.

Round 4 (Color C): Change yarn color and attach at a corner space. Ch 3, 2 dc, ch 2, 3 dc into the ch corner space. Crochet * ch 1, 3 dc, ch 1 into each of the next 2 ch spaces. 3 dc, ch 2, 3 dc into the next ch corner space * . Repeat * - * 2 more times.

Ch 1, 3 dc, ch 1 into each of the next 2 ch spaces. Attach the last ch with 1 sl st into the top of the ch 3, and crochet 2 sl sts to the ch corner space. Cut the yarn and pull it completely through.

Round 5 (Color D): Change yarn color and attach at a corner space. Ch 3, 2 dc, ch 2, 3 dc into ch corner space. Crochet * ch 1, 3 dc, ch 1 into each of the next 3 ch spaces. 3 dc, ch 2, 3 dc in the next ch corner space * . Repeat * - * 2 more times. Ch 1, 3 dc, ch 1 into each of the next 3 ch spaces. Attach the last ch with 1 sl st into the top of the ch 3, and crochet 2 sl sts to the ch corner space, but do not cut the yarn.

Round 6 (Color D): Ch 3, 2 dc, ch 2, 3 dc in ch corner space. Crochet * ch 1, 3 dc, ch 1 into each of the next 4 ch spaces. 3 dc, ch 2, 3 dc into the next ch corner space * . Repeat * – * 2 more times. Ch 1, 3 dc, ch 1 into each of the next 4 ch spaces. Attach the last ch with 1 sl st into the top of the ch 3, and crochet 2 sl sts to the ch corner space. Cut the yarn and pull it completely through.

Finishing: Weave in all loose ends and sew or crochet the squares together using whatever method you prefer. Finish the throw by crocheting a border around the entire throw using 3 dc, ch 1 into each ch space, and 3 dc, ch 2, 3 dc into each ch corner space. Repeat, 2 or 3 more rounds.

"The difficult is a trifle, the impossible a challenge."

Solan Gundersen

SHORT
Snuggle Socks

Sock Size: One Size

Yarn: Fingering #1. *Shown here:* Sisu from Sandnes Garn (80% wool, 20% nylon)

Main Color (MC):   100 grams brown no. 3161

Color A: 50 grams white no. 1001

Alternative Yarn: Rauma Finullgarn (100% wool) – dk gray heather 405, white 400

Needles: One set of five double-pointed needles size US 3 (3.25 mm)

Gauge: 28 sts and 28 rows = 4" (10 cm) stockinette

Note: The ribbing on this sock makes it very elastic, so it will fit an adult or a child's foot equally well. All you have to do is adjust the length.

Using MC and double-pointed needles, CO 60 sts on and distribute evenly across 4 needles. Join and k1, p1 for 3 rounds. On the next round pick up A and begin knitting the pattern according to the Short Snuggle Socks Chart. Knit 2 rounds in MC only. Knit the next round as follows: * Knit sts together, yo *. Repeat * – * across the round. Knit another 4 rounds. Turn your work inside out, so that the purl side is on the outside. On the next round, k2, p2 until your work measures about 8" – 10" (20 – 25 cm), or until you have the length you want, before starting on the heel.

Heel: Place the sts from the 1st and the 4th needles on one needle 30 sts total. You may choose to hold the yarn doubled for a sturdier heel. Knit back and forth (knit a row, purl a row) until you have a flap measuring 2⅜" (6 cm) then decrease as follows: knit until you have 9 sts remaining on the left needle, turn and purl until you have 9 sts remaining on the left needle. You should now have 3 sections on your needles: 9 sts, 12 sts, 9 sts, with a space in between each — 30 sts total. Turn and knit until you have 1 st before the space, sl1, k1, psso to right needle. Turn and purl until you have 1 st left before the space and 2 tog across the space. (Always leave the same number of sts on each side.) Continue decreasing in this until you reach the end of each row.

Foot: Pick up 15 sts along the side of the heel flap, k2, p2 across the instep stitches, pick up 15 stitches along the other side of the heel flap, knit across the remaining heel stitches. Join and proceed knitting in the round (k2, p2 for the instep stitches, knit only for the sole stitches).

Toe: Knit until you have 2 sts left on the first needle, sl1, k1, psso. K2tog on the second needle. Knit until you have 2 sts left on the third needle, sl1, k1, psso. K2tog on the fourth needle. Continue to decrease in this way until you have 8 sts left. Cut the yarn and pull it through the remaining sts. Weave in all loose ends.

Finishing: Steam the socks carefully using a damp kitchen towel. Fold the cuff so that the picot edging shows.

Short Snuggle Socks Chart

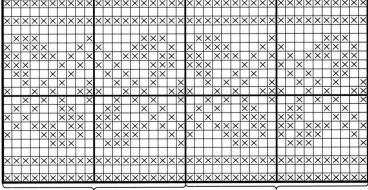

20-st repeat x 3   20-st repeat x 3

16" x 16"

Square Patterned Pillow

Finished Size: Approximately 16" x 16" (40 cm x 40 cm)

Yarn: Fingering #1. *Shown here:* Sisu from Sandnes Garn (80% wool, 20% nylon)

Main Color (MC): 200 grams brown no. 3082

Color A: 100 grams white no. 1001

Alternative Yarn: Rauma Finullgarn (100% wool) – dk brown 422, white 400

Needle: One 24" (60 cm) circular needle size US 10 (6 mm)

Gauge: 19 sts and 20 rows = 4" (10 cm) stockinette with yarn doubled

Notions: 16" x 16" (40 cm x 40 cm) down pillow insert

Holding MC doubled, CO 160 sts. Pick up A, join, and knit 2 rounds. Following Square Patterned Pillow Chart, knit 6 10-row Drop 1 MC strand and pick up A. Following Pattern Chart, knit 6 10-row repeats and then finish as shown. Knit 2 rounds in MC. BO and weave in all loose ends.

Finishing: The pillow will look the best if you hand stitch the openings shut using double yarn. Doing this will also make it easy to open the seam when you want to wash the pillow cover. A down pillow insert will make the pillow especially soft and nice. Standard 16" x 16" (40 cm x 40 cm) down filled pillow inserts are easy to find at hobby shops and fabric stores.

Square Patterned Pillow

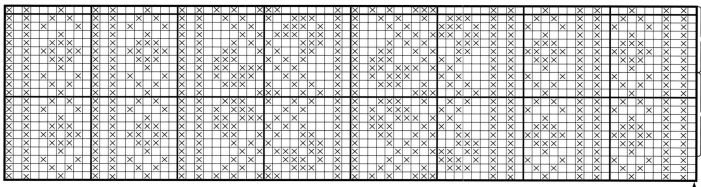

80-st repeat x 2

Finish with these eight rows

10-row repeat

Start here

Seat Cushion

Finished Size: Approximately 18" x 16" (45 cm x 40 cm)
Yarn: Fingering #1. *Shown here:* Sisu from Sandnes Garn (80% wool, 20% nylon)
Main Color (MC): 100 grams dark brown no. 3082
Color A: 100 grams white no. 1001
Alternative Yarn: Rauma Finullgarn (100% wool) – dk brown 422, white 400
Needles: One 32" (80 cm) circular needle size US 3 (3.25 mm)
Gauge: 28 sts and 28 rows = 4" (10 cm) stockinette
Notions: ¼" (0.5 cm) thick foam rubber insert

Using MC, CO 232 sts. Join and knit 2 rounds. On the next round, pick up A and begin following the Seat Cushion Chart. The seat cushion has 4 28-st repeats for the top and 4 28-st repeats for the bottom. Knit 9 10-row repeats for the length. Finish according to the chart, and then knit 2 rounds in MC. BO and weave in all loose ends.

Finishing: Lightly steam your knit cover with a damp kitchen towel. Turn the cover inside out, and stitch the top and bottom openings closed. Leave a small opening in 1 of the seams so that you can turn the knit cover back to right side out. Cut a piece of foam rubber to fit the seat cushion, and place it inside the knit cover. Hand stitch the opening closed.

Seat Cushion Chart

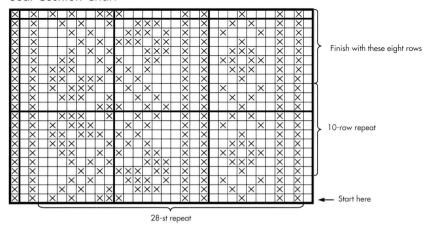

Finish with these eight rows

10-row repeat

← Start here

28-st repeat

What inspires me . . .

Summer Colors

COLORFUL
Crochet Throw

Finished Size: About 45¼" x 88⅝" (115 cm x 225 cm)

Yarn: Fingering #1. *Shown here:* Sisu from Sandnes Garn (80% wool, 20% nylon)

Colors: Approximately 225 grams each of pink no. 4517, purple no. 5226, orange no. 3308, yellow no. 2117, turquoise no. 6733, and green no. 8514

Alternative Yarn: Rauma Finullgarn (100% wool) – fuschia 456, dk royal purple 442, orange 4205, yellow 412, deep marine blue 4505, yellow green 455

Crochet Hook: One size US C-2 or D-3 (2.75 or 3.25 mm)

Note: I deliberately chose these fresh, happy colors for a blast of energy! These colors are inspiring to use and fascinating to look at. Choose your colors randomly as you work. No two squares should look alike.

INSTRUCTIONS FOR CROCHETING A GRANNY SQUARE:

Chain (ch) 4 stitches and slip stitch (sl st) into the first stitch (st) to form a ring.

Round 1 (Color A): Ch 3, 2 dc into the ring * ch 2, 3 dc into the same ring*. Repeat * - * 2 times. Ch 2. Attach the last ch with 1 sl st into the top of the ch 3, 2 sl sts to ch corner space. You have now made a small square with 4 corners.

Round 2 (Color A): Ch 3, 2 dc, ch 2, 3 dc into ch corner space * ch 1, 3 dc, ch 2, 3 dc into the next ch corner space *. Repeat * - * 2 more times. Ch 1. Attach the last ch with 1 sl st into the top of the ch 3, and 2 sl sts to the ch corner space. Cut the yarn and pull the thread all the way through.

Round 3 (Color B): Change yarn color and attach at a corner space. Ch 3, 2 dc, ch 2, 3 dc into ch corner space. Crochet * ch 1, 3 dc into next ch space, ch 1, 3 dc, ch 2, 3 dc in the next ch corner space *. Repeat * - * 2 more times. Ch 1, 3 dc into ch space, ch 1. Attach the last ch with 1 sl st into the top of the ch 3, and crochet 2 sl sts to the ch corner space. Cut the yarn and pull it completely through.

Round 4 (Color C): Change yarn color and attach at a corner space. Ch 3, 2 dc, ch 2, 3 dc into the ch corner space. Crochet * ch 1, 3 dc, ch 1 into each of the next 2 ch spaces. 3 dc, ch 2, 3 dc into the next ch corner space *. Repeat * - * 2 more times.

Ch 1, 3 dc, ch 1 into each of the next 2 ch spaces. Attach the last ch with 1 sl st into the top of the ch 3, and crochet 2 sl sts to the ch corner space. Cut the yarn and pull it completely through.

Round 5 (Color D): Change yarn color and attach at a corner space. Ch 3, 2 dc, ch 2, 3 dc into ch corner space. Crochet * ch 1, 3 dc, ch 1 into each of the next 3 ch spaces. 3 dc, ch 2, 3 dc in the next ch corner space * . Repeat * - * 2 more times. Ch 1, 3 dc, ch 1 into each of the next 3 ch spaces. Attach the last ch with 1 sl st into the top of the ch 3, and crochet 2 sl sts to the ch corner space, but do not cut the yarn.

Round 6 (Color D): Ch 3, 2 dc, ch 2, 3 dc in ch corner space. Crochet * ch 1, 3 dc, ch 1 into each of the next 4 ch spaces. 3 dc, ch 2, 3 dc into the next ch corner space * . Repeat * − * 2 more times. Ch 1, 3 dc, ch 1 into each of the next 4 ch spaces. Attach the last ch with 1 sl st into the top of the ch 3, and crochet 2 sl sts to the ch corner space. Cut the yarn and pull it completely through.

Finishing: Weave in all loose ends and sew or crochet the squares together using whatever method you prefer. Finish the throw by crocheting a border around the entire throw using 3 dc, ch 1 into each ch space, and 3 dc, ch 2, 3 dc into each ch corner space. Repeat, 2 or 3 more rounds.

DECORATIVE
Bed Pillows

16" x 24"

Finished Size: Approximately 16" x 24" (40 cm x 60 cm)

Yarn: Fingering #1. *Shown here:* Sisu from Sandnes Garn (80% wool, 20% nylon)

Material: About 300 grams (MC), about 200 grams Color A

Pillows shown on p. 102 were knit in the following color combinations:

Color Combo 1: pink no. 4517 (MC) with purple no. 5226 (Color A)

Color Combo 2: turquoise no. 6733 (MC) with green no. 8514 (Color A)

Color Combo 3: orange no. 3308 (MC) with yellow no. 2117 (Color A)

Color Combo 4: green no. 8514 (MC) with turquoise no. 6733 (Color A)

Alternative Yarn: Rauma Finullgarn (100% wool) – (1) fuschia 456, dk royal purple 442; (2) deep marine blue 4505, yellow green 455; (3) orange 4205, yellow 412; (4) yellow green 455, deep marine blue 4505

Needle: One 32" (80 cm) circular needle size US 10 (6 mm)

Gauge: 19 sts and 20 rows = 4" (10 cm) stockinette with yarn doubled

Holding MC doubled, CO 236 sts. Join and knit 2 rounds. Drop 1 strand of MC and pick up A. Begin knitting following the Decorative Bed Pillow Chart. Knit 6 10-row repeats, and finish knitting following the chart. Drop A and pick up another strand of MC. Holding yarn double, knit 2 rounds. BO and weave in loose ends.

Finishing: The pillow will look the best if you close the openings by hand stitching with the yarn doubled. It will also make it easier to open the seam when you need to wash the cover. A down pillow insert will make the pillow especially nice and soft. Standard sized 16" x 24" (40 cm x 60 cm) pillow inserts. It is also possible to use a larger pillow insert measuring 20" x 26" (50 cm x 70 cm).

Decorative Bed Pillow Chart

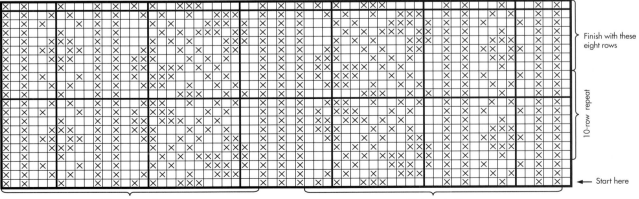

Finish with these eight rows

10-row repeat

← Start here

28-st repeat x 2   28-st repeat x 2

SHORT Snuggle Socks

Finished Size: One Size
Yarn: Fingering #1. *Shown here:* Sisu from Sandnes Garn (80% wool, 20% nylon)
Main Color (MC): 100 grams pink no. 4517
Color A: 50 grams purple no. 5226
Alternative Yarn: Rauma Finullgarn (100% wool) – fuschia 456, dk royal purple 442
Needles: One set of five double-pointed needles size US 3 (3.25 mm)
Gauge: 28 sts and 28 rows = 4" (10 cm) stockinette

Using MC and double-pointed needles, CO 60 sts on and distribute evenly across 4 needles. Join and k1, p1 for 3 rounds. On the next round pick up A and begin knitting the pattern according to the Short Snuggle Socks Chart. Knit 2 rounds in MC only. Knit the next round as follows: * Knit sts together, yo *. Repeat * – * across the round. Knit another 4 rounds. Turn your work inside out, so that the purl side is on the outside. On the next round, k2, p2 until your work measures about 8" – 10" (20 – 25 cm), or until you have the length you want, before starting on the heel.

Heel: Place the sts from the 1st and the 4th needles on one needle 30 sts total. You may choose to hold the yarn doubled for a sturdier heel. Knit back and forth (knit a row, purl a row) until you have a flap measuring 2⅜" (6 cm) then decrease as follows: knit until you have 9 sts remaining on the left needle, turn and purl until you have 9 sts remaining on the left nee-

dle. You should now have 3 sections on your needles: 9 sts, 12 sts, 9 sts, with a space in between each — 30 sts total. Turn and knit until you have 1 st before the space, sl1, k1, psso to right needle. Turn and purl until you have 1 st left before the space and 2 tog across the space. (Always leave the same number of sts on each side.) Continue decreasing in this until you reach the end of each row.

Foot: Pick up 15 sts along the side of the heel flap, k2, p2 across the instep stitches, pick up 15 stitches along the other side of the heel flap, knit across the remaining heel stitches. Join and proceed knitting in the round (k2, p2 for the instep stitches, knit only for the sole stitches).

Toe: Knit until you have 2 sts left on the first needle, sl1, k1, psso. K2tog on the second needle. Knit until you have 2 sts left on the third needle, sl1, k1, psso. K2tog on the fourth needle. Continue to decrease in this way until you have 8 sts left. Cut the yarn and pull it through the remaining sts. Weave in all loose ends.

Finishing: Steam the socks carefully using a damp kitchen towel. Fold the cuff so that the picot edging shows.

Short Snuggle Socks Chart

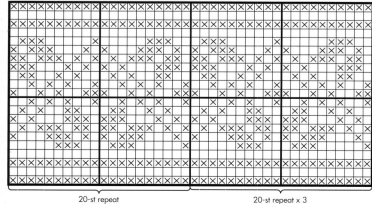

20-st repeat   20-st repeat x 3

Knee-High Sock Chart S

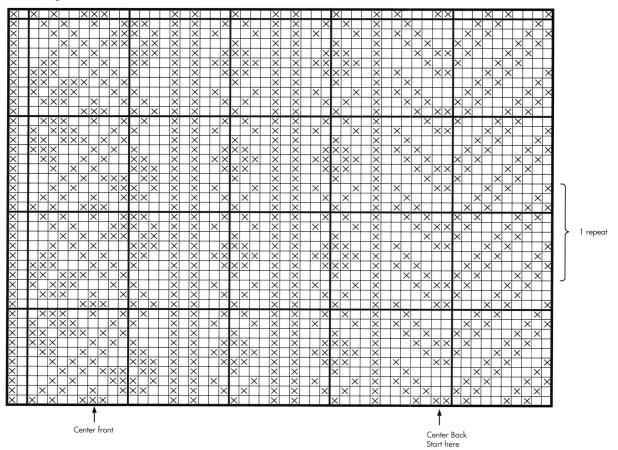

1 repeat

Center front

Center Back
Start here

Chart A

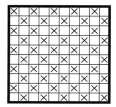

KNEE-HIGH
Snuggle Socks

Sizes: S (M, L)

Finished Lengths: 13¾ (17, 19¾)" (35 (43, 50) cm) long

Yarn: Fingering #1. *Shown here:* Sisu from Sandnes Garn (80% wool, 20% nylon)

Quantity: 100 (100,150) grams MC; 50 (50, 100) grams Color A

Color Combo 1:   orange no. 3308 (MC) with yellow no. 2117 (Color A)

Color Combo 2:   green no. 8514 (MC) with turquoise no 6733 (Color A)

Alternative Yarn: Rauma Finullgarn (100% wool) – (1) orange 4205, yellow 412
    (2) yellow green 455, deep marine blue 4505

Needles: One set of five double-pointed needles size US 3 (3.25 mm)

Gauge: 28 sts and 28 rows = 4" (10 cm) stockinette

CO 64 (72, 80) sts in MC and distribute evenly over 4 dpns. Join and k1, p1 for 2⅜" (2¾, 2¾)" (6 (7, 7) cm). On the next round, knit in stockinette, increasing by 5 sts evenly distributed across the round — sts 69 (77, 85). Knit pattern following the Knee-High Sock Chart for the size you are knitting (center back is the same for all sizes) until your work measures about 7⅛" (8⅝", 10¼)" (18 (22, 26) cm). Decrease 1 st at the beginning and the end of every 4th round at center back, until you have 48 (58, 62) sts. Continue to knit pattern until your work measures 13 (17, 19⅝)" (35 (43, 50) cm) or your desired length.

Heel: Make the heel using sts from the first and the fourth needle placed on to 1 needle, 24 (28, 30) sts total. Holding MC double, knit back and forth (knitting and purling) until you have a flap measuring 2 (2⅜, 2⅜)" 95 (6, 6) cm), then decrease to turn the heel: knit until you have 7 (8, 9) sts remaining on the left needle, turn, and purl until you have 7 (8, 9) sts remaining on the left needle, PM. You should now have three sections on your needles: 7 (8, 9) sts, 10 sts, 7 (8, 9) sts, with a marker in between each — 24 sts. Turn, again, and knit until you have

1 st before the space. Sl1, k1, psso, turn, and purl until you have 1 st left before the space and p2tog. (Always leave the same number of sts on each side.) Continue decreasing in this manner on every row until you have 12 (14, 15) sts. Pick up 12 (14, 15) sts on each side of the heel, join with the top sts. Continue knitting in pattern across the instep, and knit the sole following Chart A. Knit until the foot measures about 6 (8, 8⅝)" (16 (20, 22) cm), or is at a desired length, before starting to decrease for the toe.

Toe: Knit all sts following Chart A. Decrease for the toe at each side of the foot by knitting until you have 2 sts left on the first needle, sl1, k1, psso. K2tog at the beginning of the second needle. Knit until you have 2 sts remaining on the third needle, sl1, k1, psso. K2tog at the beginning of the fourth needle. Continue decreasing on each round until you have 8 sts remaining. Cut the yarn and pull the it through the remaining sts. Weave in all loose ends.

Steam the socks carefully with an iron, using a damp kitchen towel.

Knee-High Sock Chart M

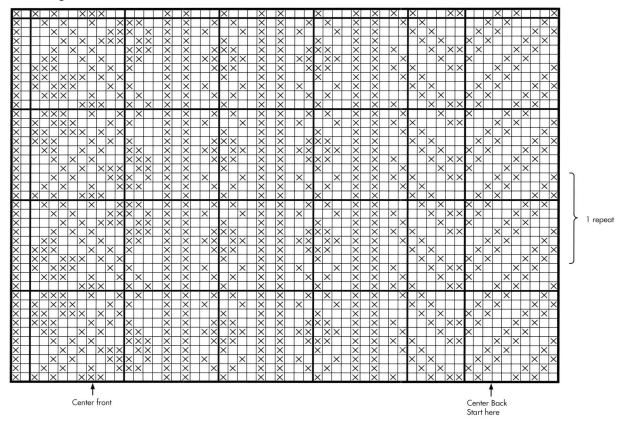

1 repeat

Center front

Center Back
Start here

Chart A

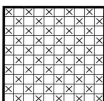

Knee-High Sock Chart L

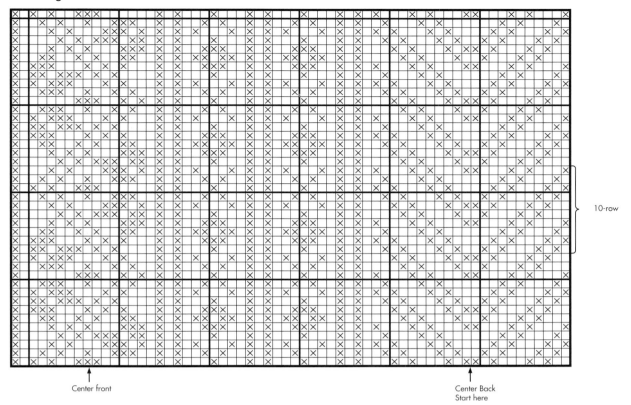

Center front

Center Back
Start here

10-row

Chart A

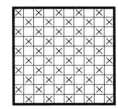

Square Patterned Pillow

16" x 16"

Finished Size: Approximately 16" x 16" (40 cm x 40 cm)

Yarn: Fingering #1. *Shown here:* Sisu from Sandnes Garn (80% wool, 20% nylon)

Main Color (MC): 200 grams orange no. 3308

Color A: 200 grams yellow no. 2117

Alternative Yarn: Rauma Finullgarn (100% wool) – orange 4205, yellow 412

Needle: One 24" (60 cm) circular needle size US 10 (6 mm), 24" (60 cm) long

Gauge: 19 sts and 20 rows = 4" (10 cm) double yarn

Notions: 16" x 16" (40 cm x 40 cm) down pillow insert

Holding MC doubled, CO 160 sts. Pick up A, join, and knit 2 rounds. Following Square Patterned Pillow Chart, knit 6 10-row Drop 1 MC strand and pick up A. Following Pattern Chart, knit 6 10-row repeats and then finish as shown. Knit 2 rounds in MC. BO and weave in all loose ends.

Finishing: The pillow will look the best if you hand stitch the openings shut using double yarn. Doing this will also make it easy to open the seam when you want to wash the pillow cover. A down pillow insert will make the pillow especially soft and nice. Standard 16" x 16" (40 cm x 40 cm) down filled pillow inserts are easy to find at hobby shops and fabric stores.

Square Patterned Pillow Chart

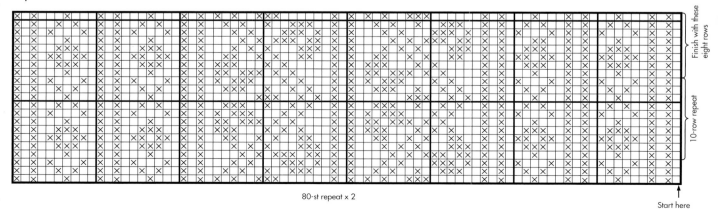

80-st repeat x 2

Finish with these eight rows

10-row repeat

Start here

Bow Tie

Finished Size: Approximately 5½" x 2¾" (14 cm x 7 cm)

Yarn: Fingering #1. *Shown here:* Sisu from Sandnes Garn (80% wool, 20% nylon)

Main Color (MC): 50 grams turquoise no. 6733

Color A: 50 grams green no. 8514

Alternative Yarn: Rauma Finullgarn (100% wool) – deep marine blue 4505, yellow green 455

Needles: One set of five double-pointed needles size US 3 (3.25 mm)

Gauge: 28 sts and 28 rows = 4" (10 cm) stockinette

Notions: String, ⅝" (1.5 cm) wide velvet ribbon or similar, velcro

CO 42 sts in MC and distribute evenly over 4 needles. Join and knit 2 rounds, then pick up A and continue knitting following the Bow Tie Front Chart. Needles 1 and 4 are knit according to Bow Tie Back Chart, and needles 2 and 3 are knit according to Bow Tie Front Chart.

Knit two 20-row repeats for the length — about 6¼" (16 cm). Knit 2 rounds in MC. BO and weave in all loose ends.

Steam lightly with a damp kitchen towel.

Finishing: Turn your knit piece inside out and sew a seam at each end, leaving a small opening at one end so that you can turn the piece right-side out. Sew the small opening shut, by hand, on the right side of the bow.

Tie string tightly around the middle of the bow. Then knit a "cover" to conceal the string. CO 6 sts knit stockinette until your work measures 2" (5 cm). BO. Place the knit strip over the string, and attach it to the back of the bow. Measure the neck of the bow's recipient, cut a ribbon a little longer than the measured size, and attach it to the bow. I used a ⅝" (1.5 cm) wide velvet ribbon. Attach velcro, for closure, to the ends of the ribbon.

Bow Tie Front Chart

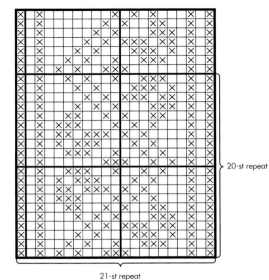

21-st repeat

20-st repeat

Bow Tie Back Chart

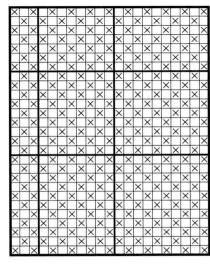

21-st repeat

Guide to Abbreviations

Knitting Abbreviations	
BO	bind off
CO	cast on
dpns	double-pointed needles
k	knit
k2tog	knit two together
MC	main color
p	purl
psso	pass slipped stitch over
p2tog	purl two together
sl	slip
st	stitch
yo	yarn over

Crochet Abbreviations	
ch	chain
dc	double crochet
sc	single crochet
sl st	slip stitch
sp	space
st	stitch

Resources

Following are sources (both online and in-store) for the
Sandnes Sisu and Fritidsgarn yarn used in *Yarn Happy*.
Contact these companies for materials.

USA
- Swedish Yarn
  www.swedishyarn.com
  P.O. Box 2069
  Jamestown, North Carolina 27282
  Phone: (800) 331-5648
  Fax: (336) 887-6702
  E-mail: info@swedishyarn.com
  Ships worldwide, carries Sisu only

- Yarn and Fiber
  www.yarnandfiber.com
  Address: 14 East Broadway
  Derry, New Hampshire 03038
  Phone: (603) 505-4432
  Ships worldwide, carries Sisu only, limited colors

CANADA
- Myrtle Station Wool & Ferguson's Knitting
  myrtlestationwool.blogspot.com
  Address: 9585 Baldwin St N., Ashburn, Ontario
  L0B 1A0, Canada
  Phone: +1 (905) 655-4858
  Store only purchases, no online shipping. Carries Sisu only

- True North Yarn Co.
  www.truenorthyarn.com
  Address: 79 Anne St S, Barrie, Ontario
  L4N 2E2, Canada
  Phone: toll-free 1 (888) 304-4418+1 (705) 737-4422
  E-mail: kelly@truenorthyarn.com
  Ships worldwide, carries Sisu and Fritidsgarn

- Needle & Arts Centre
  www.needlenart.com
  Address: 990A Shoppers Row, Campbell River, British Colombia
  Canada V9W 2C5
  Phone: +1 (250) 287-8898
  E-mail: info@needlenart.com
  Ships worldwide, carries Sisu and Fritidsgarn

- Wool-Tyme
  www.wool-tyme.com
  Address: 2-190 Colonnade Rd S., Ottawa, Ontario
  K2E 7J5, Canada
  Phone: (613) 225-9665
  E-mail: woolinfo@wool-tyme.com
  Ships worldwide, carries Sisu and Fritidsgarn

UK
- SKD Yarns
  www.skdyarns.net
  Address: Glen Rosa Stryt Isa, Penyffordd, Chester CH4 0JY, United Kingdom
  Phone: +44 (0) 1978761047
  E-mail: Sales@ScandinavianKnittingDesign.com
  Ships worldwide, carries Sisu and Fritidsgarn

If you can't find Sisu or Fritisdgarn from Sandnes Garn,
here are some yarns that are comparable

Sisu:
Machine Wash 40 degrees C, 3 ply, 50 grams = 175 m (1.76 oz = 191 yards),
80% Pure New Wool, 20% Nylon, 26 sts x 34 rows, 10 cm x 10 cm (4" x 4"),
on 2.5mm or 3 mm (US 2) needles
This is a fingering/sock weight yarn

Finullgarn from Rauma: *(see p.124)*
2 ply, 50 grams = 175 m (191 yards), 100% wool from Norway, 6-7 sts per inch
on 2.5 mm - 3.5 mm needles, size 2 (US); hand wash, lay flat to dry
Offers a large selection of colors

(continued on p. 120)

Resources (continued)

Fritidsgarn from Rauma:
3-ply bulk knitting, 50 gram ball = 80 m, 100% Norwegian wool, 4-4.5 st/in on size 5.0 mm - 5.5 mm needles; hand wash, lay flat to dry

- Nordic Fiber Arts
  www.nordicfiberarts.com
  Address: 4 Cutts Road, Durham, New Hampshire 03824
  Phone: (603) 868-1196
  E-mail: info@nordicfiberarts.com
  Offers a large selection of colors for Finullgarn and Fritidsgarn

- Ingebretsen's
  www.ingebretsens.com
  Address: 1601 E. Lake Street, Minneapolis, Minnesota 55407
  Phone: (612) 729-9333 | toll-free (800) 279-9333
  E-mail: info@ingebretsens.com
  Offers a large selection of colors for Finullgarn and Fritidsgarn

BFL Sock from Sweet Georgia:
80% superwash wool, 20% nylon, 400 yards/365 m per 4 oz/115 g skein,
US 0-1 (2 - 2.25 mm) needles
Offers a large selection of colors

Koigu Premium Yarn (KPM) from Koigu:
100% plied Merino wool, fingering, 4 ply, 175 yards (160 meters),
50 grams (1.76 ounces), 28.0 sts = 4 inches, US 2.5 - 3.0 mm needles
Offers a large selection of colors

Sock Yarn from Malabrigo:
100 grams per skein (400 yards), light fingering plied 100 % super wash Merino wool.
US 1 - 3 (2.25 mm - 3.25 mm) needles, 32 sts = 4 ", machine washable
Limited color selection

Sock Yarn from Stroll:
100 grams per skein (462 yards), fingering weight, 75% superwash Merino wool,
25% nylon, 7 - 8 sts = 1" on US 1 - 3 (2.25 mm - 3.25 mm) needles,
machine wash gentle, tumble dry low
Limited color selection

Reinforcing Heels & Toes

When knitting socks with 100% wool yarn it's a good idea to strengthen the areas that experience the most wear and tear — usually the heels and toes — with synthetic fiber thread.

Polyester thread: Buy a spool of polyester (not cotton!) sewing thread to match your main color yarn. Simply hold it together with your yarn as you knit the heel and/or toe stitches.

Reinforcement thread: This is a thin, yarn-like thread composed of superwash wool and nylon/acrylic. It can be held together with your yarn as you knit, or woven into the heel and/or toe. To weave in the thread, use a tapestry needle to simply lace it over and under the purl ridges, up and down the columns of stitches on the wrong side of your work. Lang Jawoll Reinforcement Thread is 75% Superwash Wool/ 18% Nylon/ 7% Acrylic and comes in a variety of colors.

Yarn Weights

Yarn Weight Symbol & Category Names	**0** LACE	**1** SUPER FINE	**2** FINE	**3** LIGHT
Types of Yarns in Category	Fingering 10 count crochet thread	Sock, Fingering, Baby	Sport, Baby	DK, Light Worsted
Knit Gauge* Range in Stockinette Stitch to 4 inches	33–40** sts	27–32 sts	23–26 sts	21–24 sts
Recommended Needle in Metric Size Range	1.5–2.25 mm	2.25—3.25 mm	3.25—3.75 mm	3.75—4.5 mm
Recommended Needle U.S. Size Range	000–1	1 to 3	3 to 5	5 to 7
Crochet Gauge* Ranges in Single Crochet to 4 inch	32–42 double crochets**	21–32 sts	16–20 sts	12–17 sts
Recommended Hook in Metric Size Range	Steel*** 1.6–1.4 mm	2.25—3.5 mm	3.5—4.5 mm	4.5—5.5 mm
Recommended Hook U.S. Size Range	Steel*** 6, 7, 8 Regular hook B–1	B–1 to E–4	E–4 to 7	7 to I–9

** Lace weight yarns are usually knitted or crocheted on larger needles and hooks to create lacy, openwork patterns. Accordingly, a gauge range is difficult to determine. Always follow the gauge stated in your pattern.

*** Steel crochet hooks are sized differently from regular hooks — the higher the number, the smaller the hook, which is the reverse of regular hook sizing

Yarn Weight Symbol & Category Names	4 MEDIUM	5 BULKY	6 SUPER BULKY	7 JUMBO
Types of Yarns in Category	Worsted, Afghan, Aran	Chunky, Craft, Rug	Bulky, Roving	Jumbo, Roving
Knit Gauge* Range in Stockinette Stitch to 4 inches	16–20 sts	12–15 sts	7–11 sts	6 sts and fewer
Recommended Needle in Metric Size Range	4.5—5.5 mm	5.5—8 mm	8—12.75 mm	12.75 mm and larger
Recommended Needle U.S. Size Range	7 to 9	9 to 11	11 to 17	17 and larger
Crochet Gauge* Ranges in Single Crochet to 4 inch	11–14 sts	8–11 sts	6–9 sts	5 sts and fewer
Recommended Hook in Metric Size Range	5.5—6.5 mm	6.5—9 mm	9—16 mm	16 mm and larger
Recommended Hook U.S. Size Range	I–9 to K–10 1/2	K–10 1/2 to M–13	M–13 to Q	Q and larger

Chart © 2015 Craft Yarn Council • craftyarncouncil.com/weight.html

* GUIDELINES ONLY: The above reflect the most commonly used gauges and needle or hook sizes for specific yarn categories.

Rauma Yarn Charts

RAUMA FINULLGARN
2 ply knitting and 7/2 weaving yarn
100% wool imported from Norway
175 meters/50 gram ball
6-7 st/in on size 2.5mm - 3.5mm needles

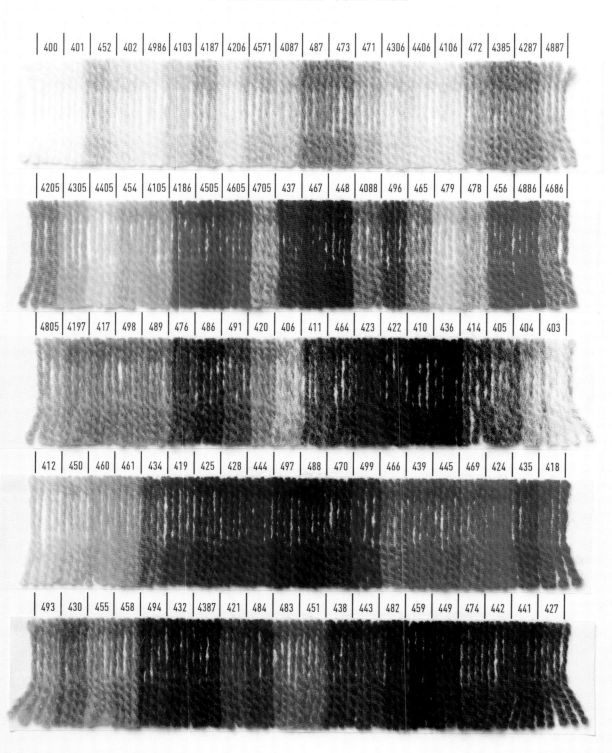

| 400 | 401 | 452 | 402 | 4986 | 4103 | 4187 | 4206 | 4571 | 4087 | 487 | 473 | 471 | 4306 | 4406 | 4106 | 472 | 4385 | 4287 | 4887 |

| 4205 | 4305 | 4405 | 454 | 4105 | 4186 | 4505 | 4605 | 4705 | 437 | 467 | 448 | 4088 | 496 | 465 | 479 | 478 | 456 | 4886 | 4686 |

| 4805 | 4197 | 417 | 498 | 489 | 476 | 486 | 491 | 420 | 406 | 411 | 464 | 423 | 422 | 410 | 436 | 414 | 405 | 404 | 403 |

| 412 | 450 | 460 | 461 | 434 | 419 | 425 | 428 | 444 | 497 | 488 | 470 | 499 | 466 | 439 | 445 | 469 | 424 | 435 | 418 |

| 493 | 430 | 455 | 458 | 494 | 432 | 4387 | 421 | 484 | 483 | 451 | 438 | 443 | 482 | 459 | 449 | 474 | 442 | 441 | 427 |

| V26 | V45 | V44 |

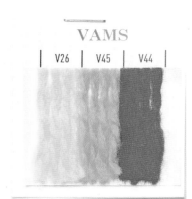

RAUMA VAMSEGARN

3-ply bulky weight knitting yarn   5/3 weaving yarn
100% wool imported from Norway
83 meters/50 gram ball
4-4.5 sts/in on size 5.0 mm - 5.5 mm needles

MÅ IKKE BLØTLEGGES

| | Temperatur inntil 150°C | Rensing i perkloretylen normal metode | Tåler ikke trommetørk | Tåler ikke klorbleking |

| V00 | V01 | V66 | V60 | V63 | V55 | V64 | V06 | V03 | V13 | V14 | V10 |

| V80 | V87 | V89 | V81 | V20 | V43 | V18 | V23 | V35 | V57 | V65 | V96 | V71 |

| V88 | V53 | V47 | V48 | V49 | V50 | V76 | V37 | V51 | V82 | V77 | V58 | V36 |

| V05 | V25 | V42 | V61 | V24 | V56 | V95 | V12 | V67 | V34 | V86 | V52 | V75 |

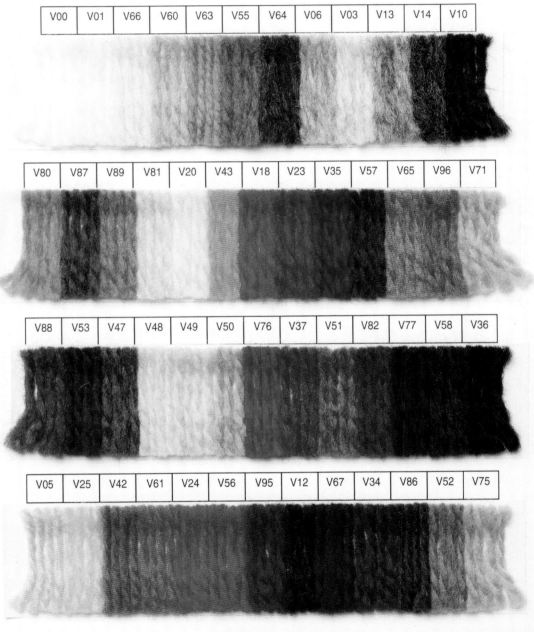

www.raumaull.no

Acknowledgments

My dream has been fulfilled. The road was long. Much work was done, but I arrived at my goal; this book is finished and I am infinitely grateful. A big thank-you goes to you, Mamma. Thank you for all the yarn ends you fastened, the granny squares you sewed together, and the finishing work you helped me complete. I couldn't have done it without you.

Sellers Publishing wishes to thank author Turid Lindeland for her beautiful work on this book, as well as everyone at Cappelen Damm for their help and assistance. Margaret Berge Hartge deserves a generous thank-you for expertly translating the book from its original Norwegian. Special thanks goes to Debbie Gremlitz of Nordic Fiber Arts in Durham, New Hampshire for sharing with us her extensive knowledge of fibers and knitting. Thanks, too, to Maya Mackowiak Elson, copyeditor extraordinaire! There wasn't a detail too small or a extra step too big that she didn't carefully review or wasn't willing to take.